My First Pet

Gerbils

by Vanessa Black

Bullfrog
Books

Ideas for Parents and Teachers

Bullfrog Books let children practice reading informational text at the earliest reading levels. Repetition, familiar words, and photo labels support early readers.

Before Reading

- Discuss the cover photo. What does it tell them?
- Look at the picture glossary together. Read and discuss the words.

Read the Book

- "Walk" through the book and look at the photos. Let the child ask questions. Point out the photo labels.
- Read the book to the child, or have him or her read independently.

After Reading

- Prompt the child to think more. Ask: What do you need to take care of a gerbil? Would you like one as a pet?

Bullfrog Books are published by Jump!
5357 Penn Avenue South
Minneapolis, MN 55419
www.jumplibrary.com

Library of Congress Cataloging-in-Publication Data

Names: Black, Vanessa, author.
Title: Gerbils / by Vanessa Black.
Description: Minneapolis, MN: Jump!, Inc., [2017]
Series: My first pet | Audience: Age 5–8.
Audience: K to grade 3. | Includes index.
Identifiers: LCCN 2016024519 (print)
LCCN 2016027195 (ebook)
ISBN 9781620315514 (hardcover: alk. paper)
ISBN 9781624964992 (ebook)
Subjects: LCSH: Gerbils as pets—Juvenile literature.
Classification: LCC SF459.G4 B53 2017 (print)
LCC SF459.G4 (ebook) | DDC 636.935/83—dc23
LC record available at https://lccn.loc.gov/2016024519

Editor: Kirsten Chang
Book Designer: Michelle Sonnek
Photo Researcher: Michelle Sonnek

Photo Credits: All photos by Shutterstock except:
Age Fotostock, 1, 5, 6–7, 10–11, 12–13, 16–17, 22, 23tl;
Alamy, 3, 4, 8–9, 15, 18, 19, 22, 23tr, 23br, 24; Kimball
Stock, 14; Superstock, 20–21.

Printed in the United States of America at
Corporate Graphics in North Mankato, Minnesota.

Table of Contents

A New Pet

Kip is at the shelter.

He sees gerbils.

Gerbils are soft.

They are fast.

They look fun!

What do they need?

Gerbils need friends.
In the wild, gerbils
live in groups.
It is best to have
two or more.

9

Gerbils need space.

They run.

They climb.

They jump.

A big cage is best.

wheel

Gerbils need exercise.

Bud and Moe have
a wheel.

They like to run.

13

Gerbils like to hide.
Red has a hut.

14

QT shares a log.

Gerbils need food.
They eat pellets.
They drink water.

pellets

shavings

Gerbils need shavings.
Emi takes out the old ones.
She puts in new ones.

Cho digs in the shavings.
Fun!

Gerbils are great pets!

What Does a Gerbil Need?

glass cage
Gerbils love to dig. Glass homes work best for gerbils because they keep shavings in.

water bottle
Gerbils chew plastic. Glass water bottles are best.

exercise wheel
A gerbil's tail can get stuck in a wire wheel. Solid floor wheels are good for gerbils.

shavings
Gerbils need a lot of wood shavings. They use them to burrow.

Picture Glossary

exercise
Physical movement that is done to be strong and healthy.

shelter
A place where people take care of animals that do not have homes.

pellets
A mix of crushed up food made into small chunks.

wild
In nature.

Index

To Learn More

Learning more is as easy as 1, 2, 3.

1) Go to www.factsurfer.com

2) Enter "petgerbils" into the search box.

3) Click the "Surf" button to see a list of websites.

With factsurfer.com, finding more information is just a click away.